Italian Girls

Hot Sexy Italian Lingerie Girls Models Pictures

By **PHOTO ART LOVER**

Copyright © Italian Girls

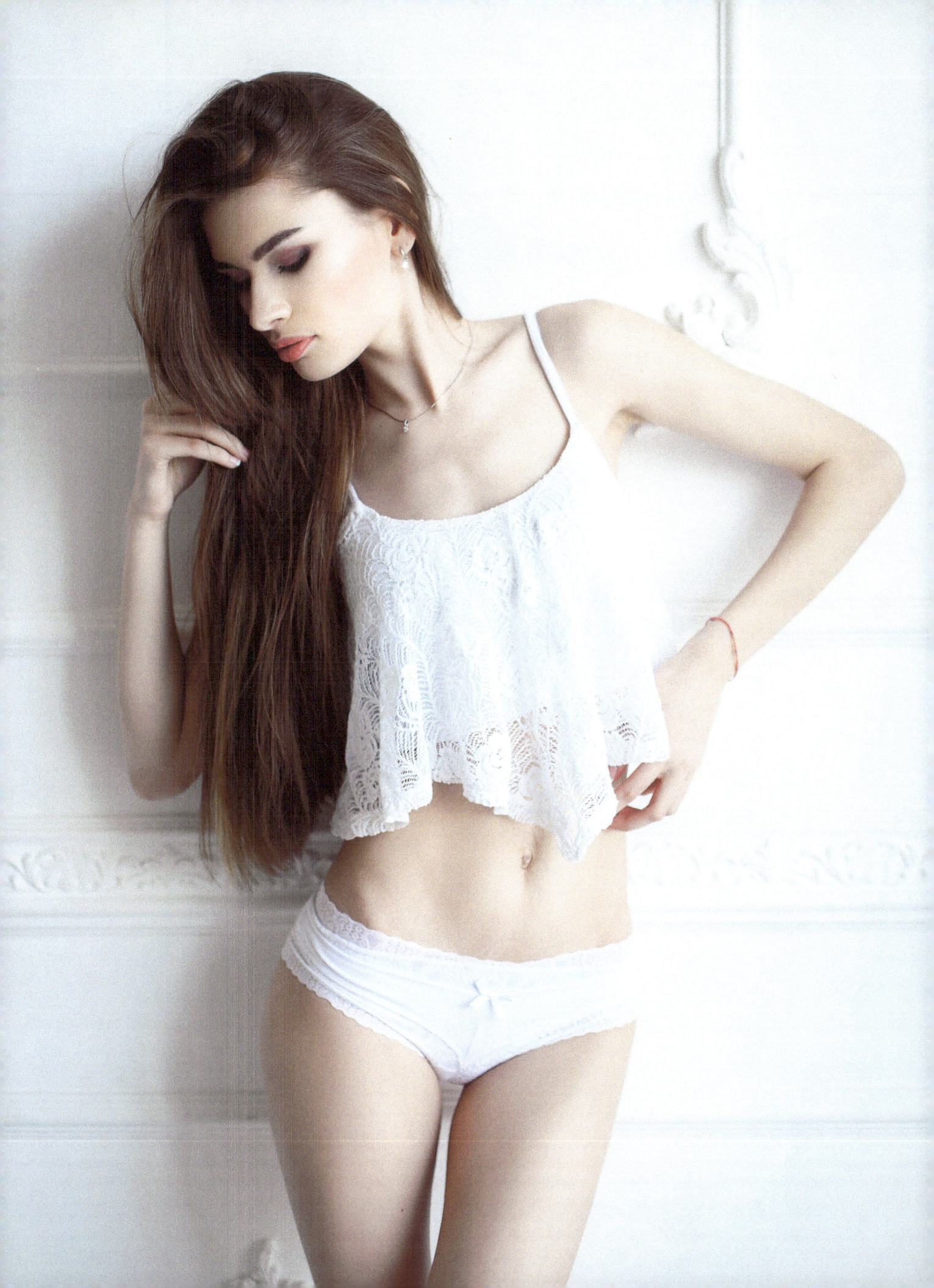

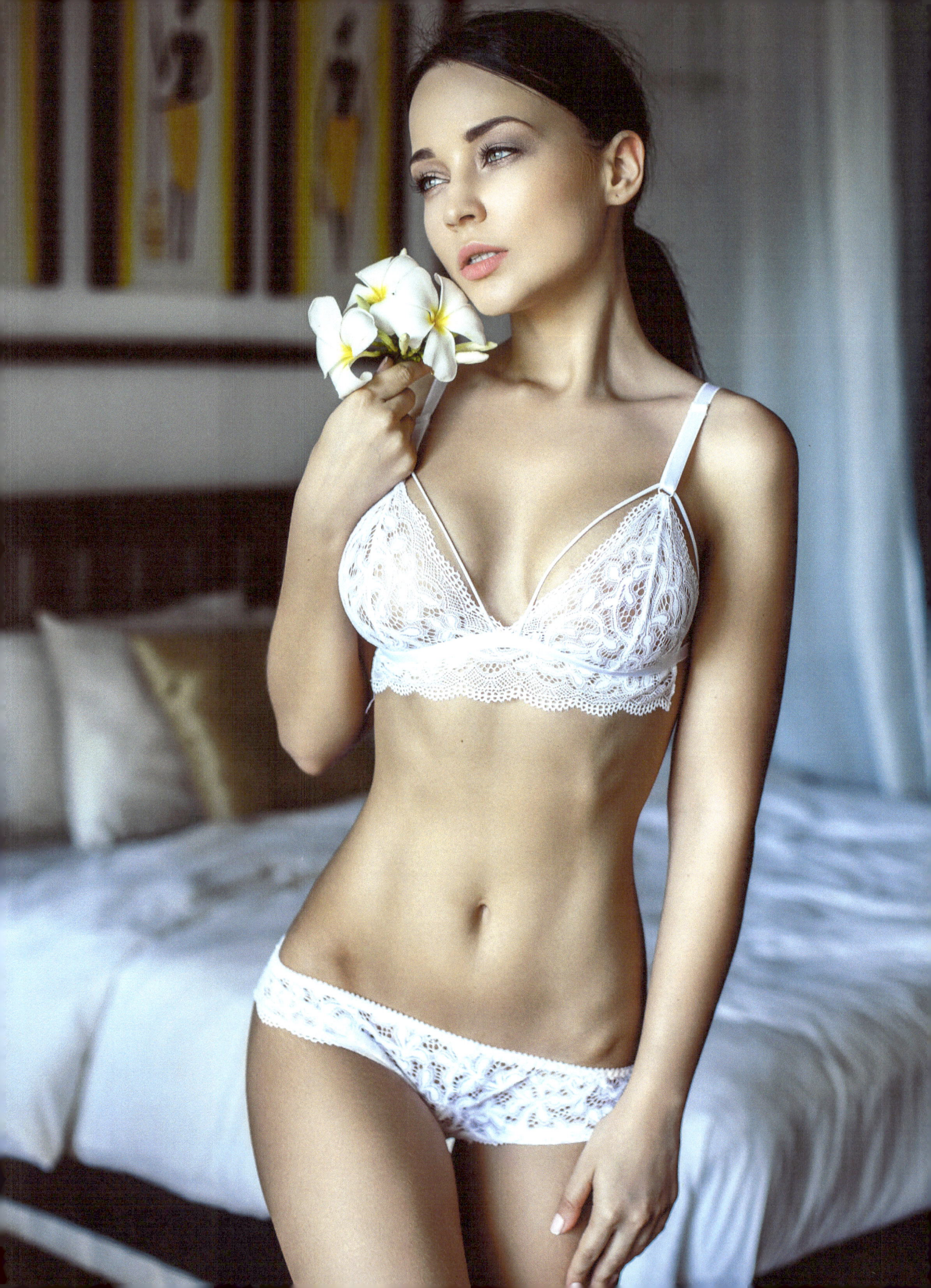

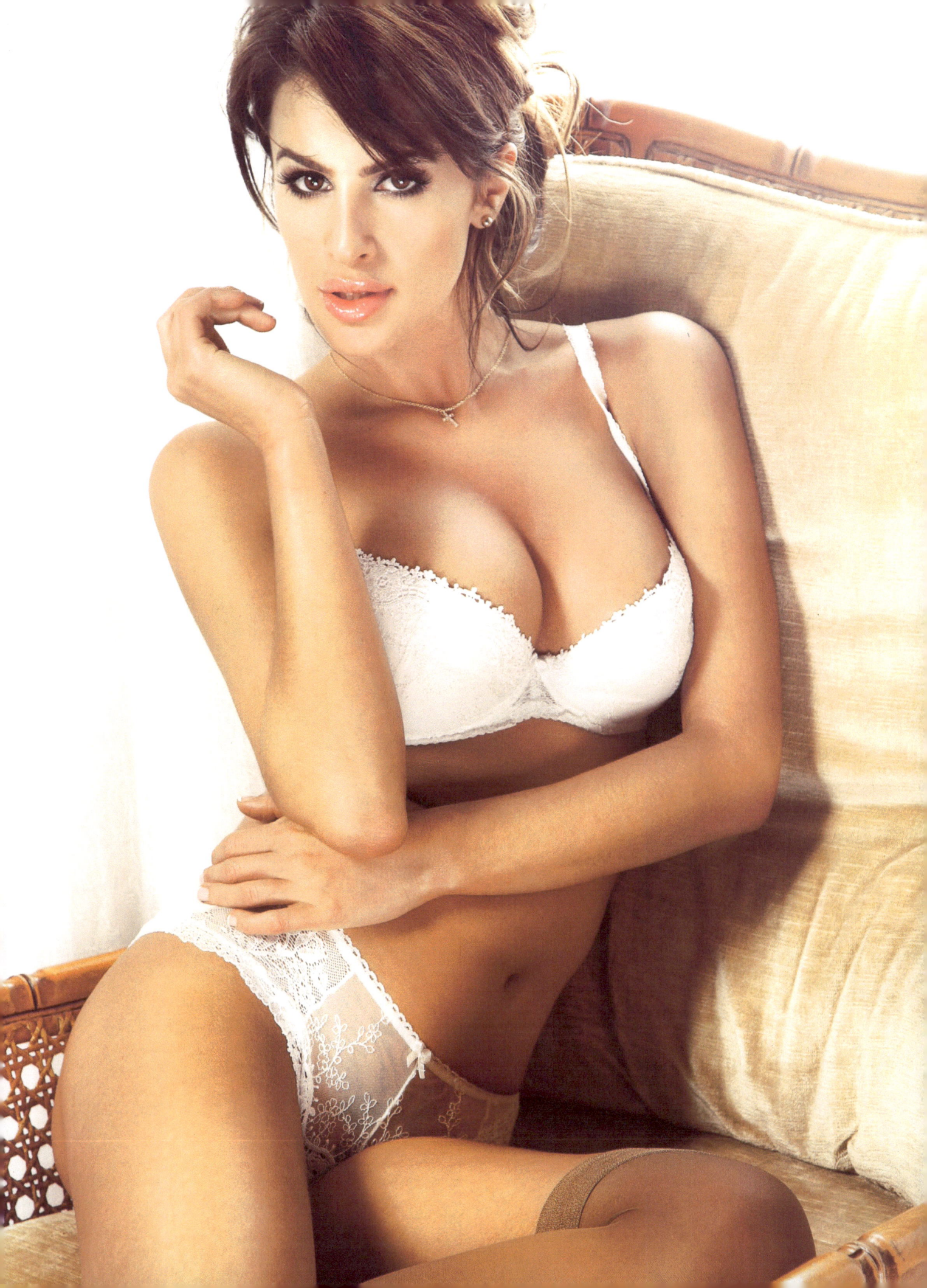

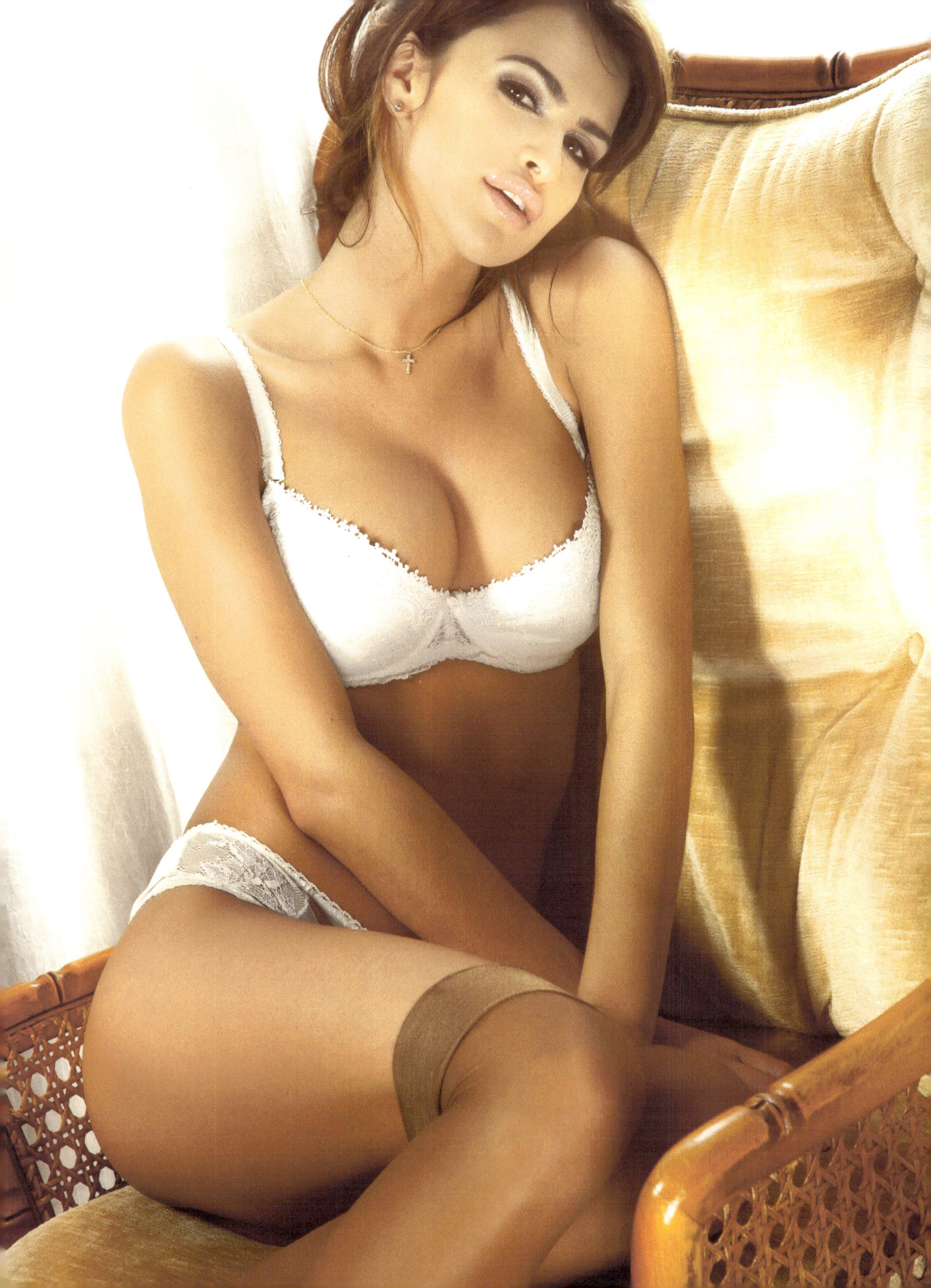

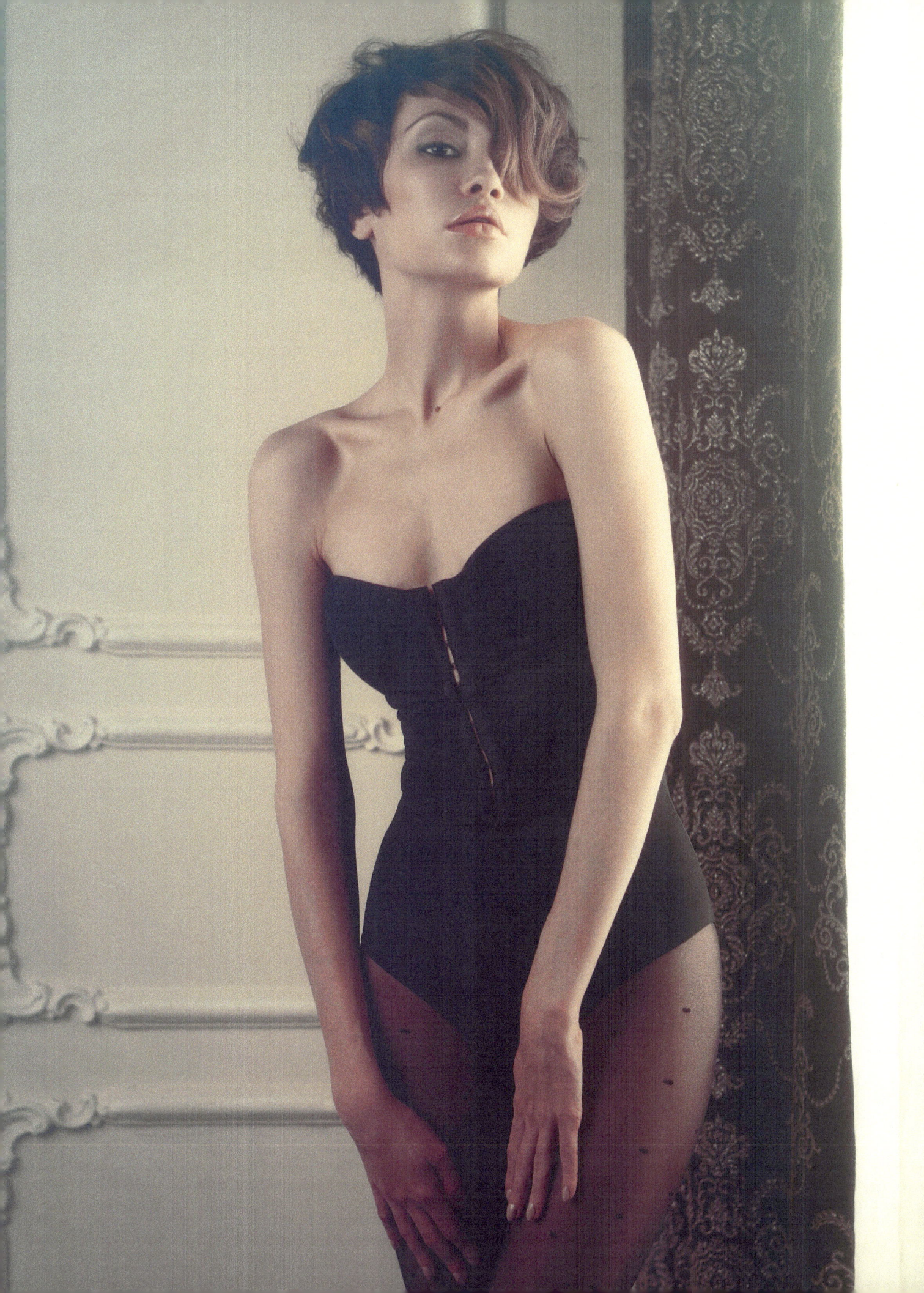

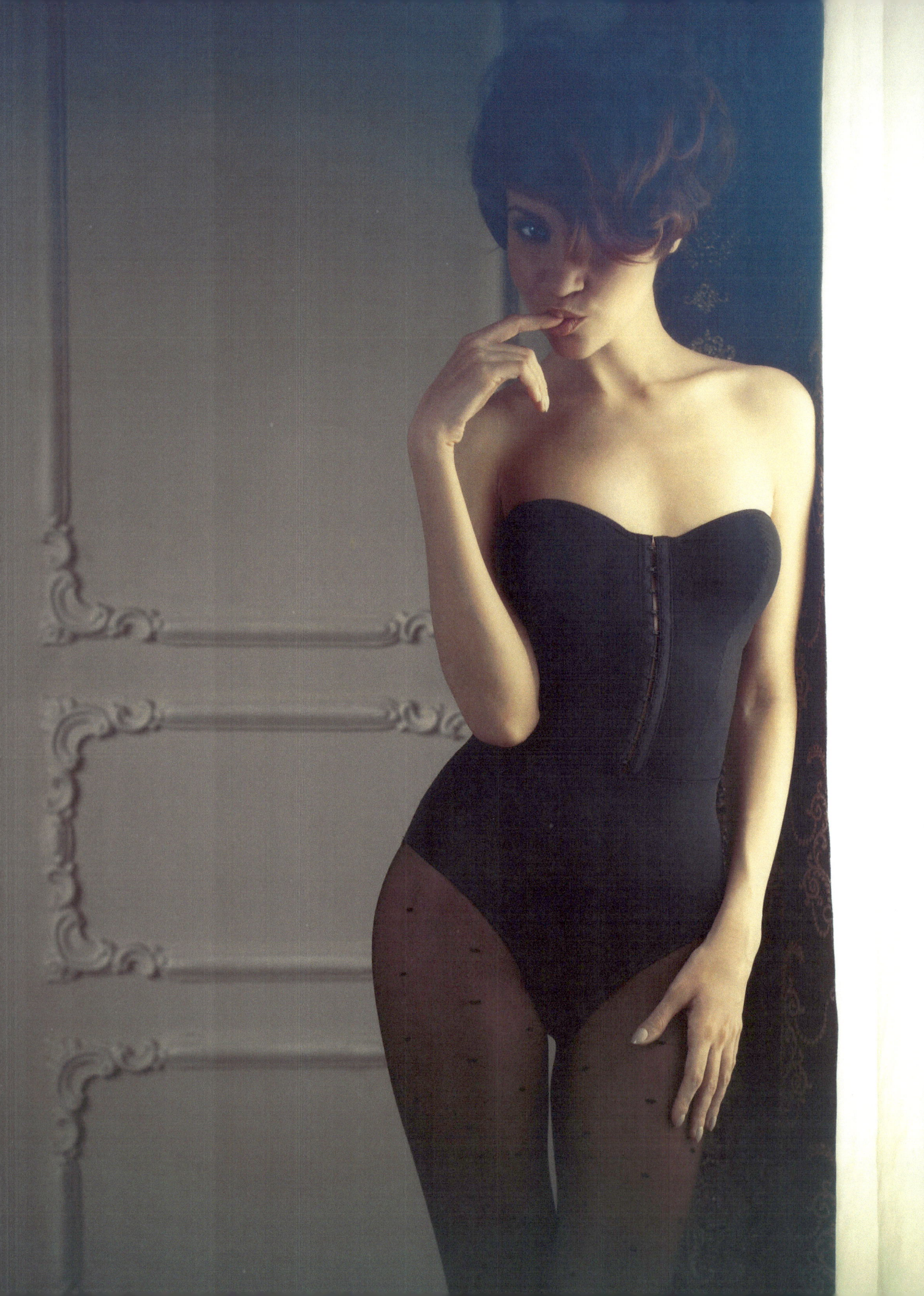

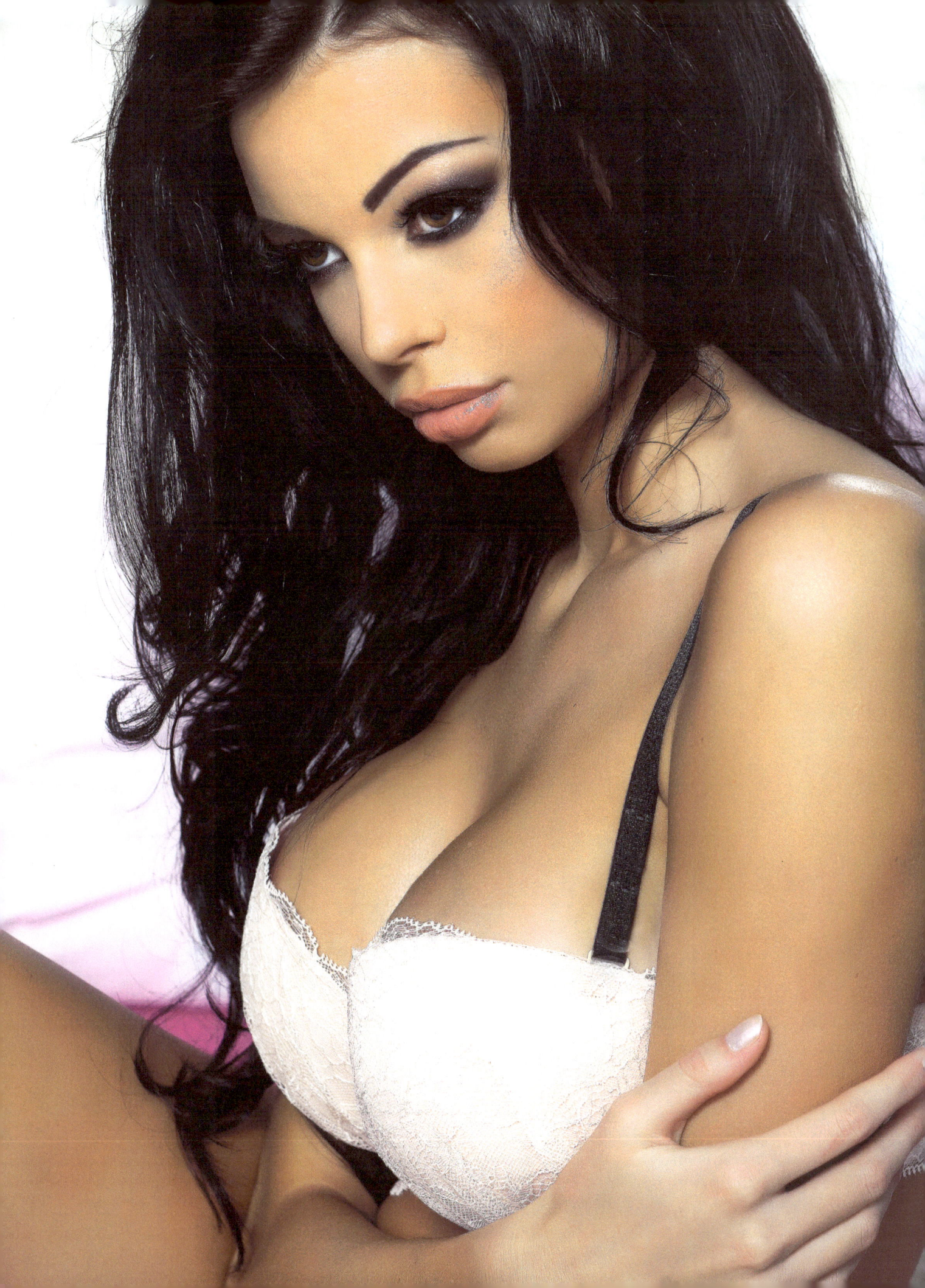

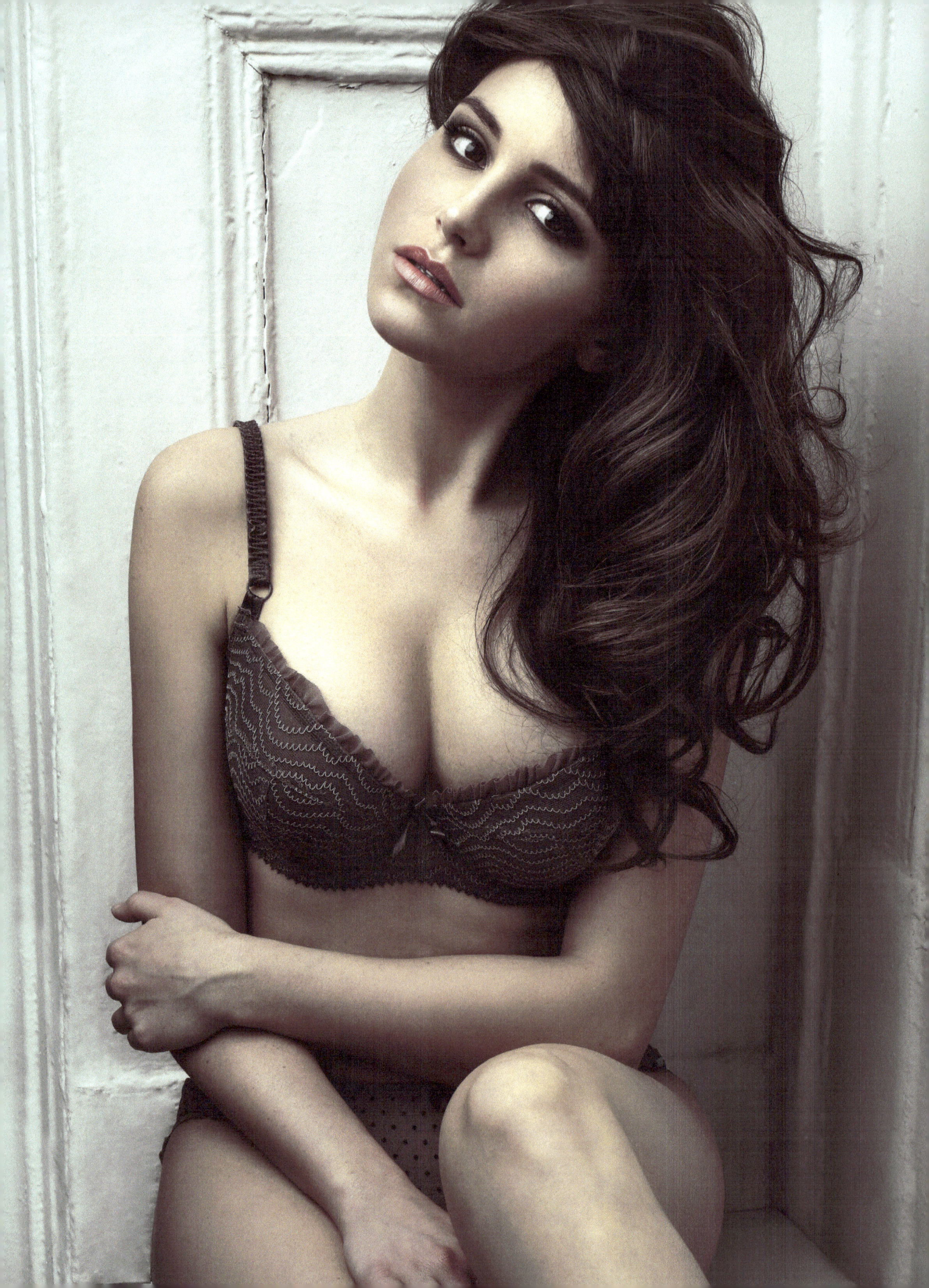

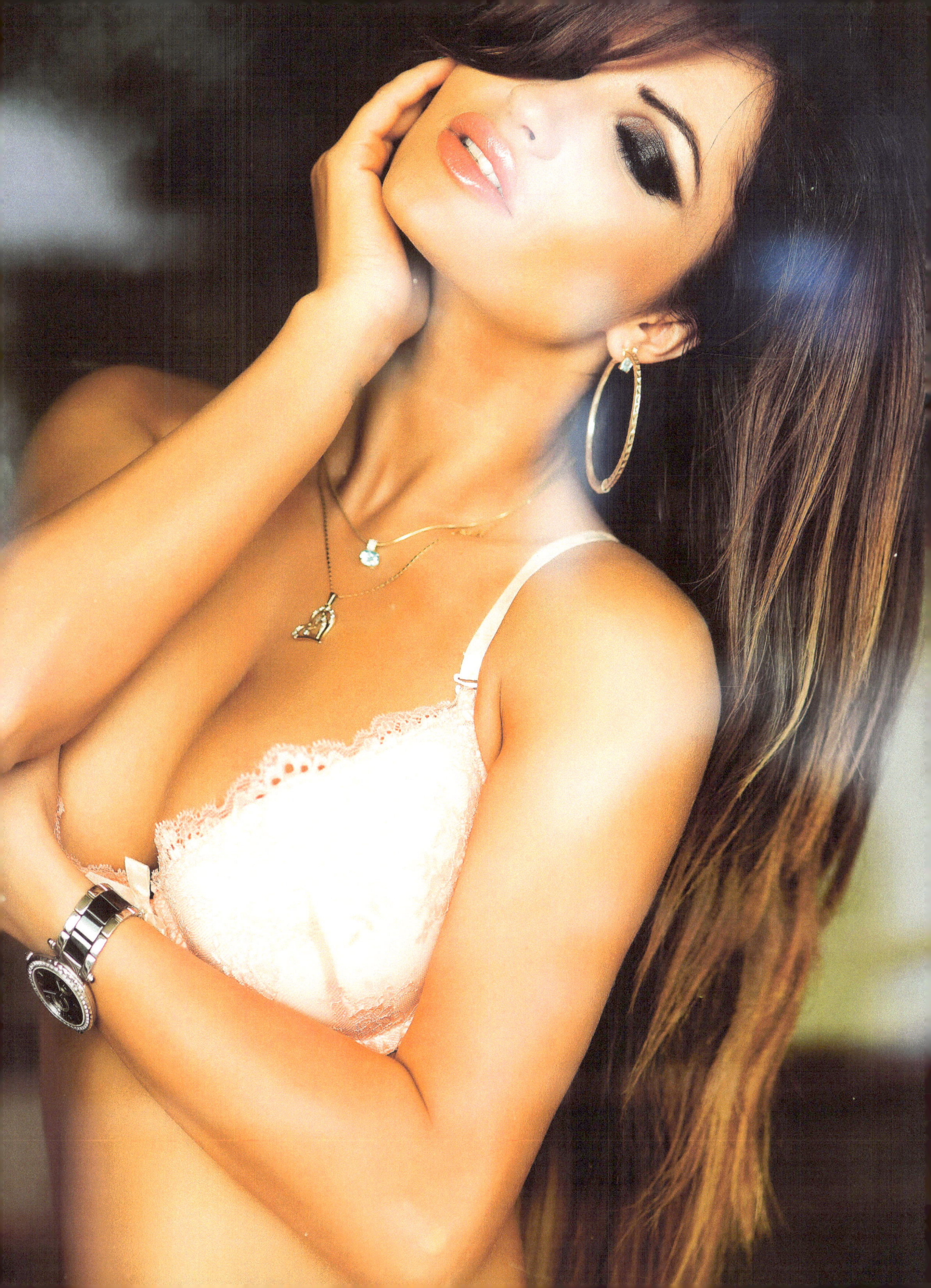

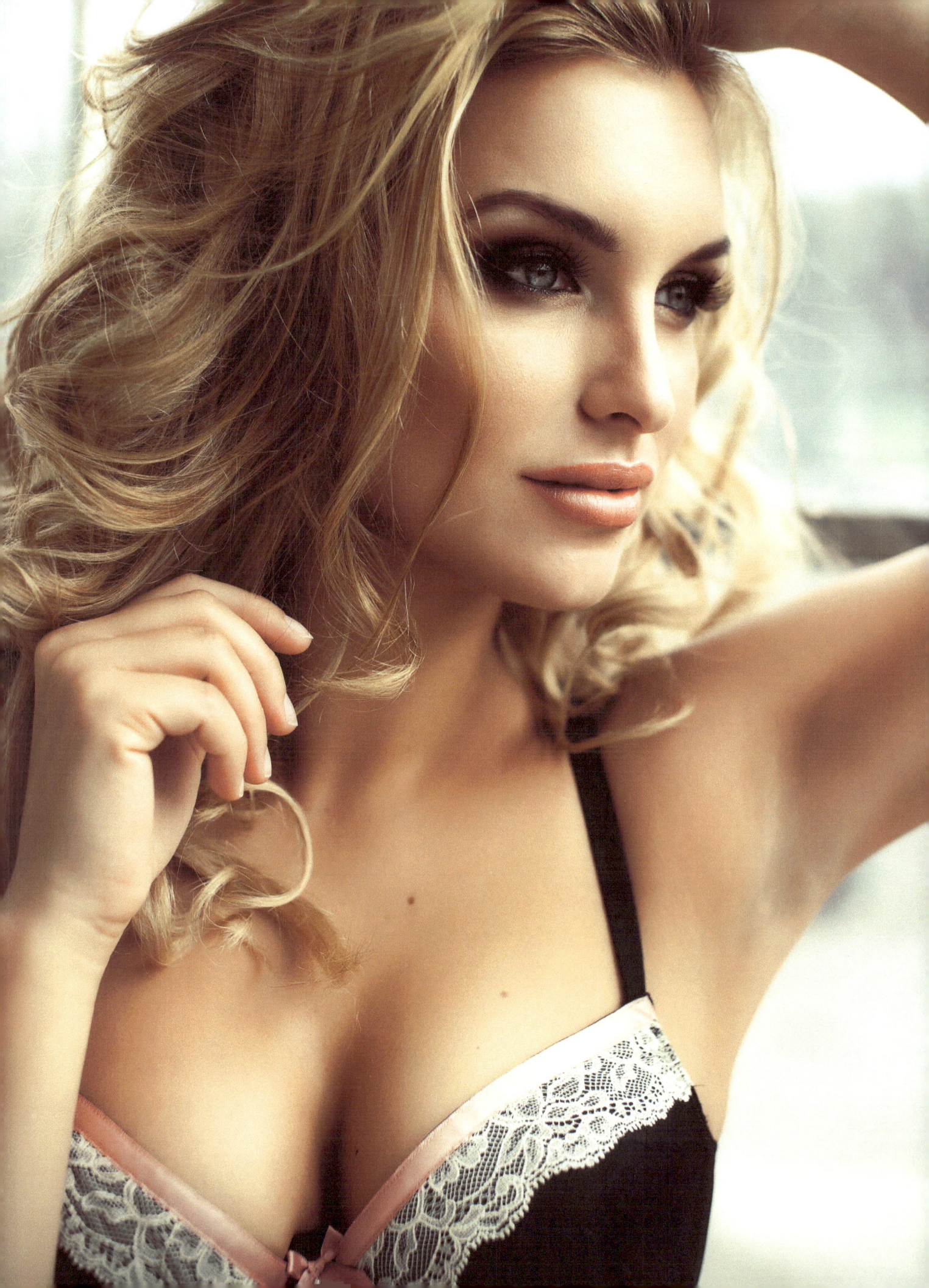

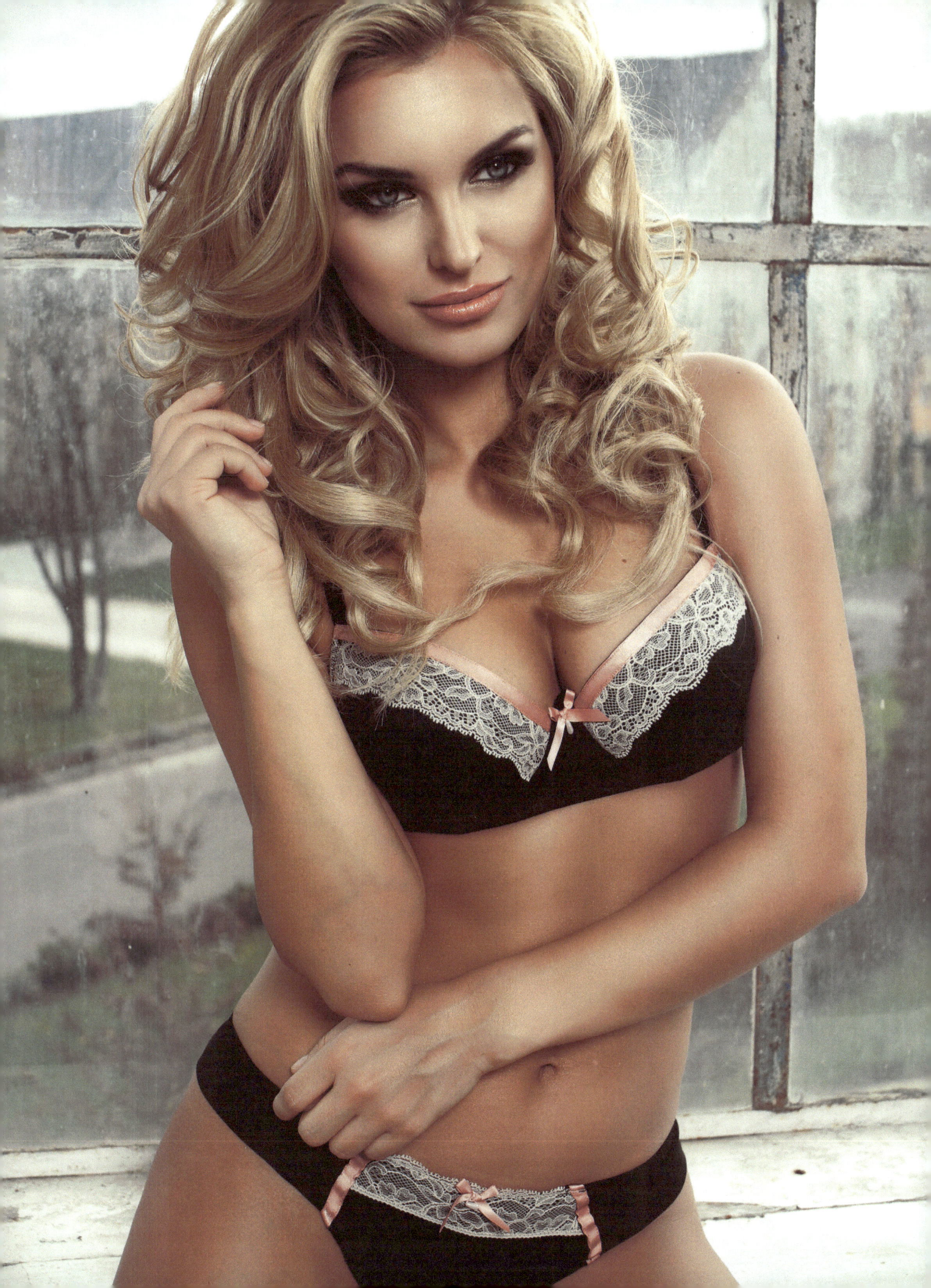

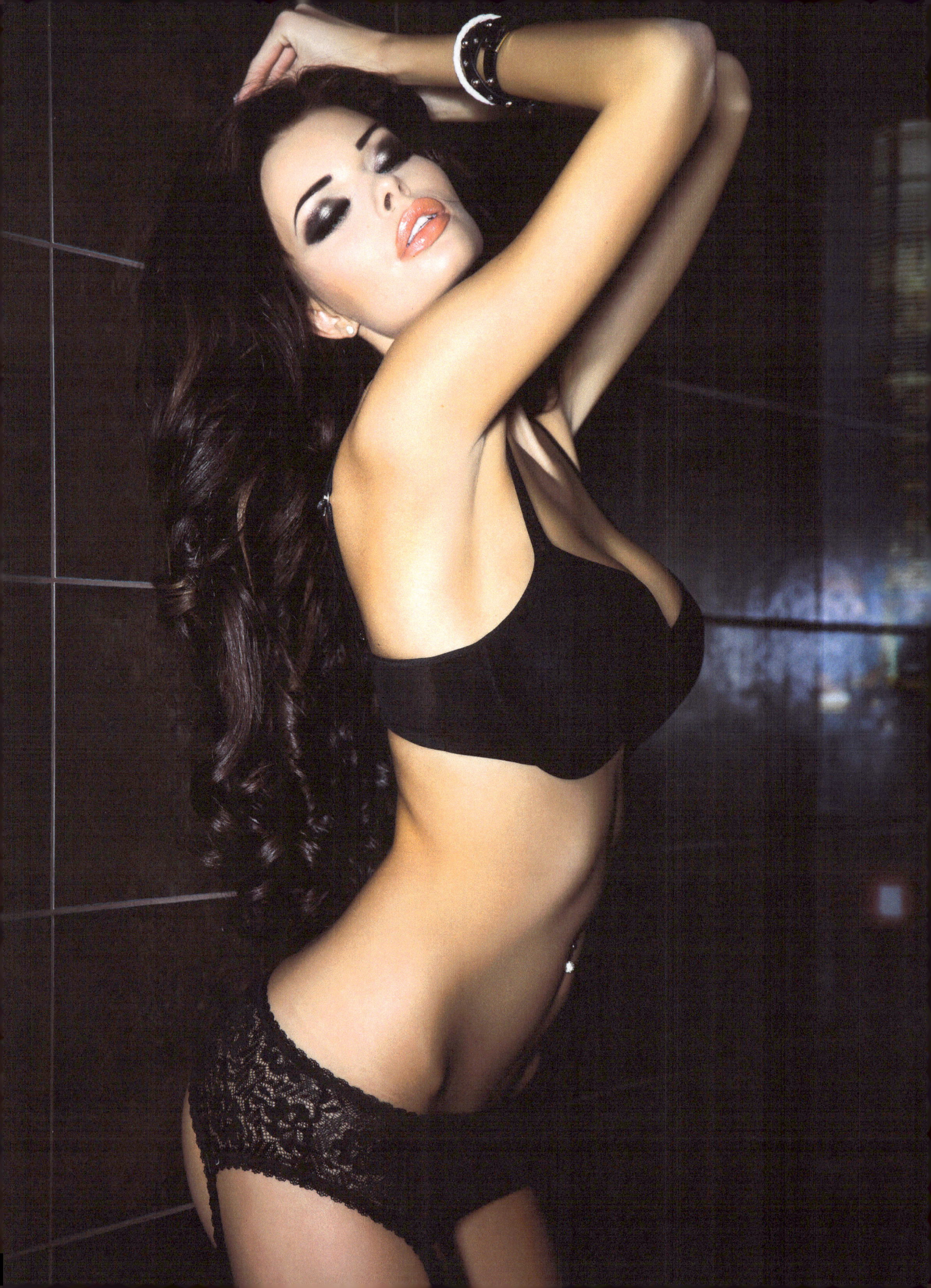

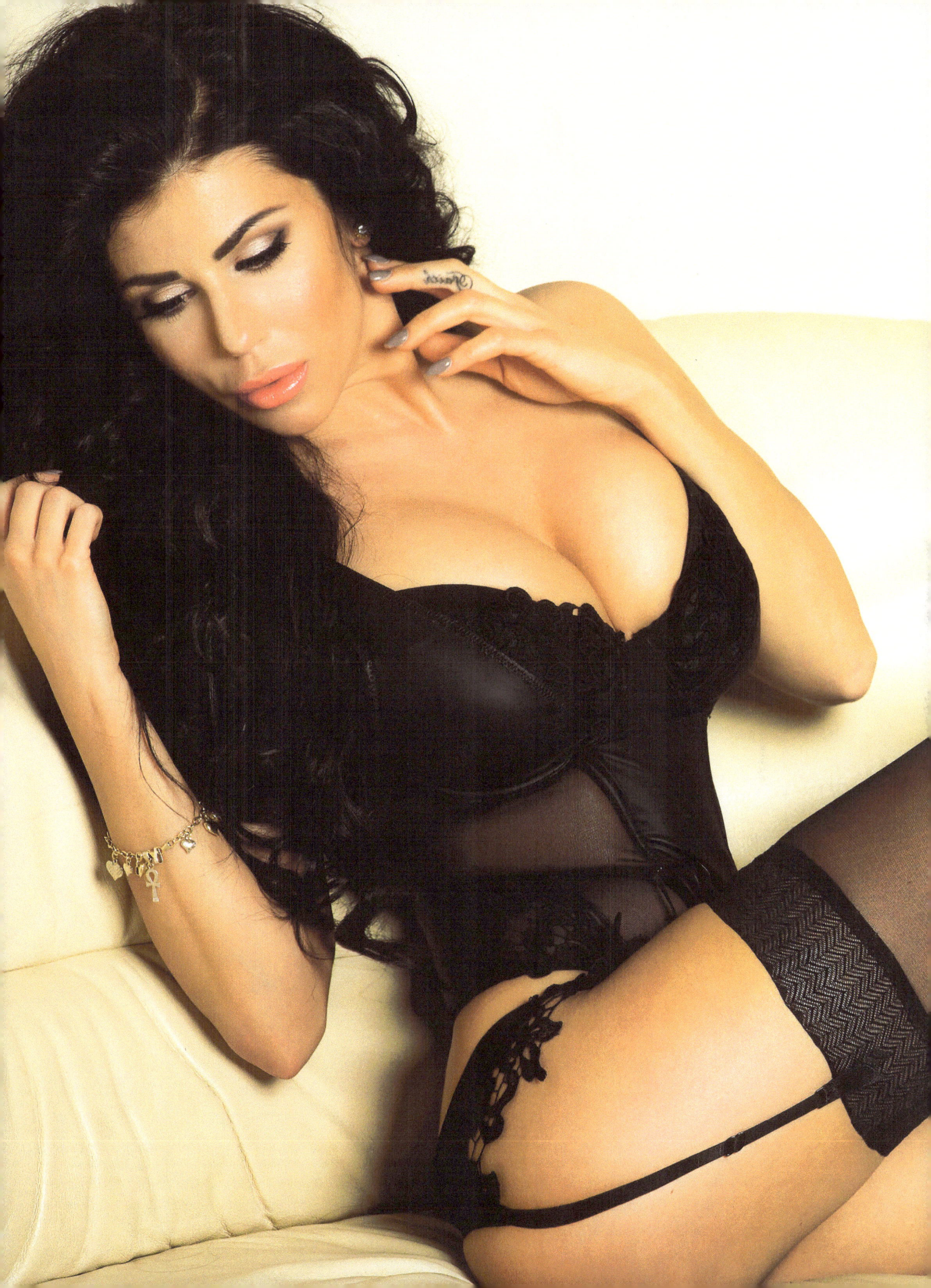

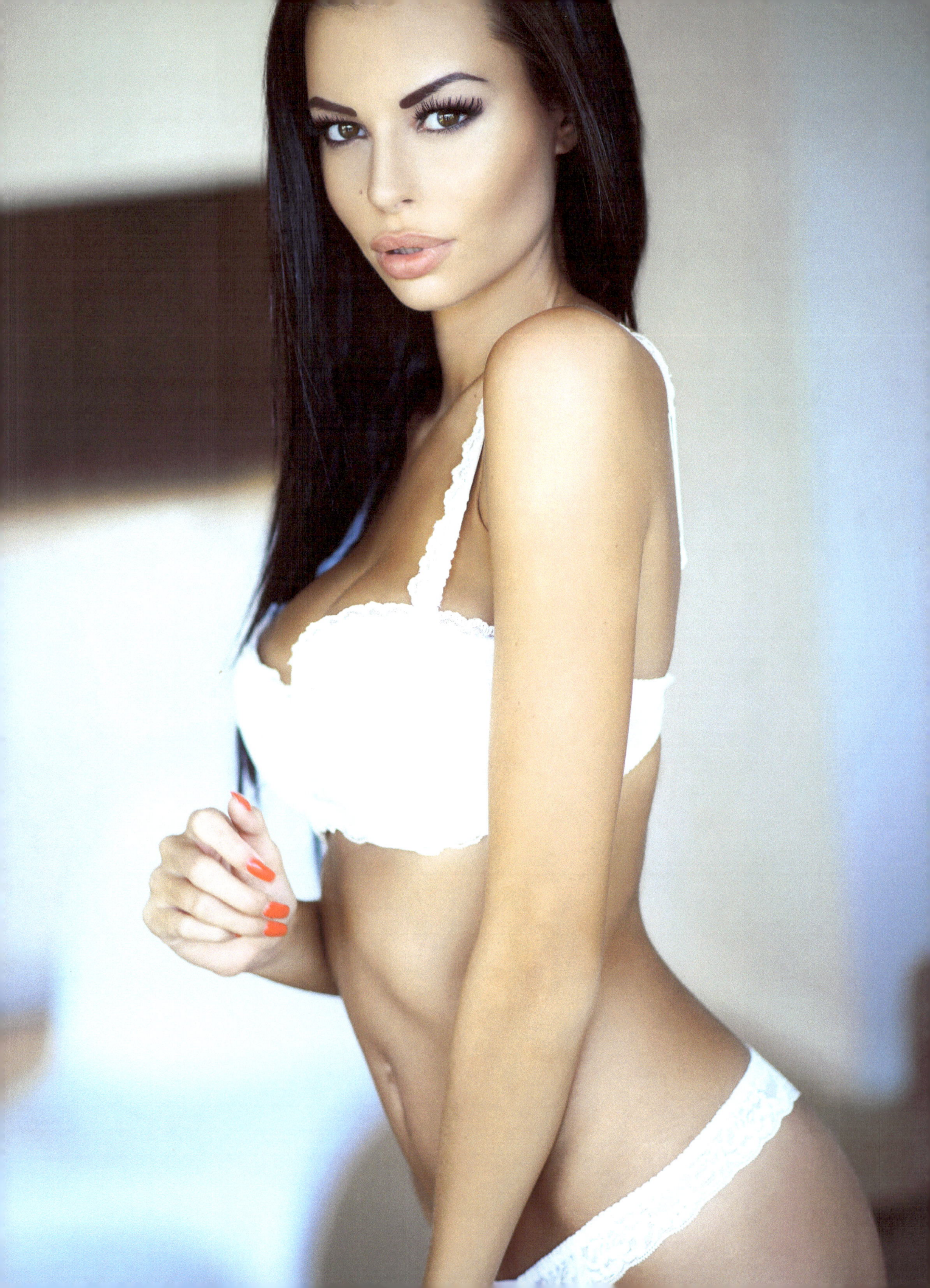

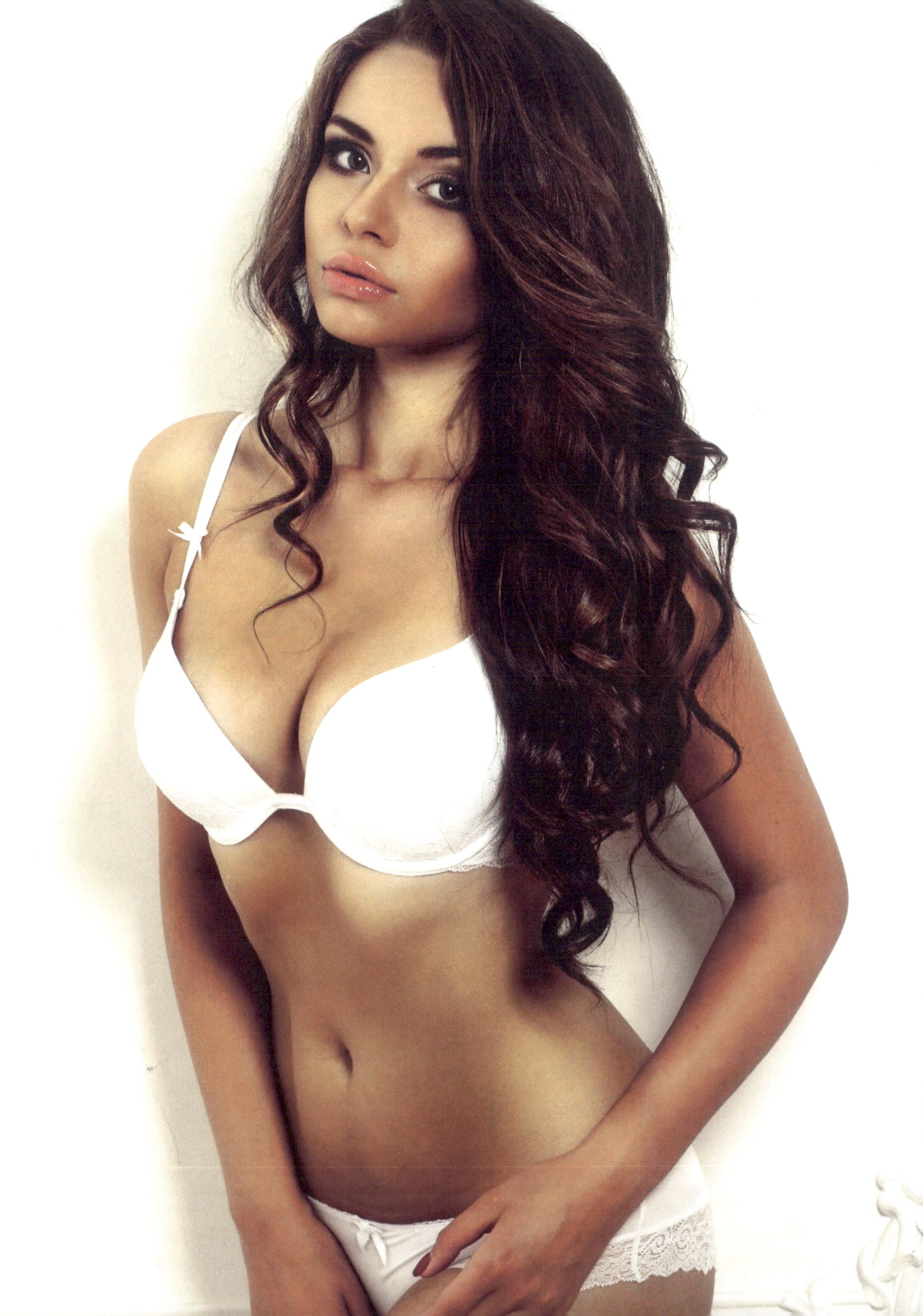

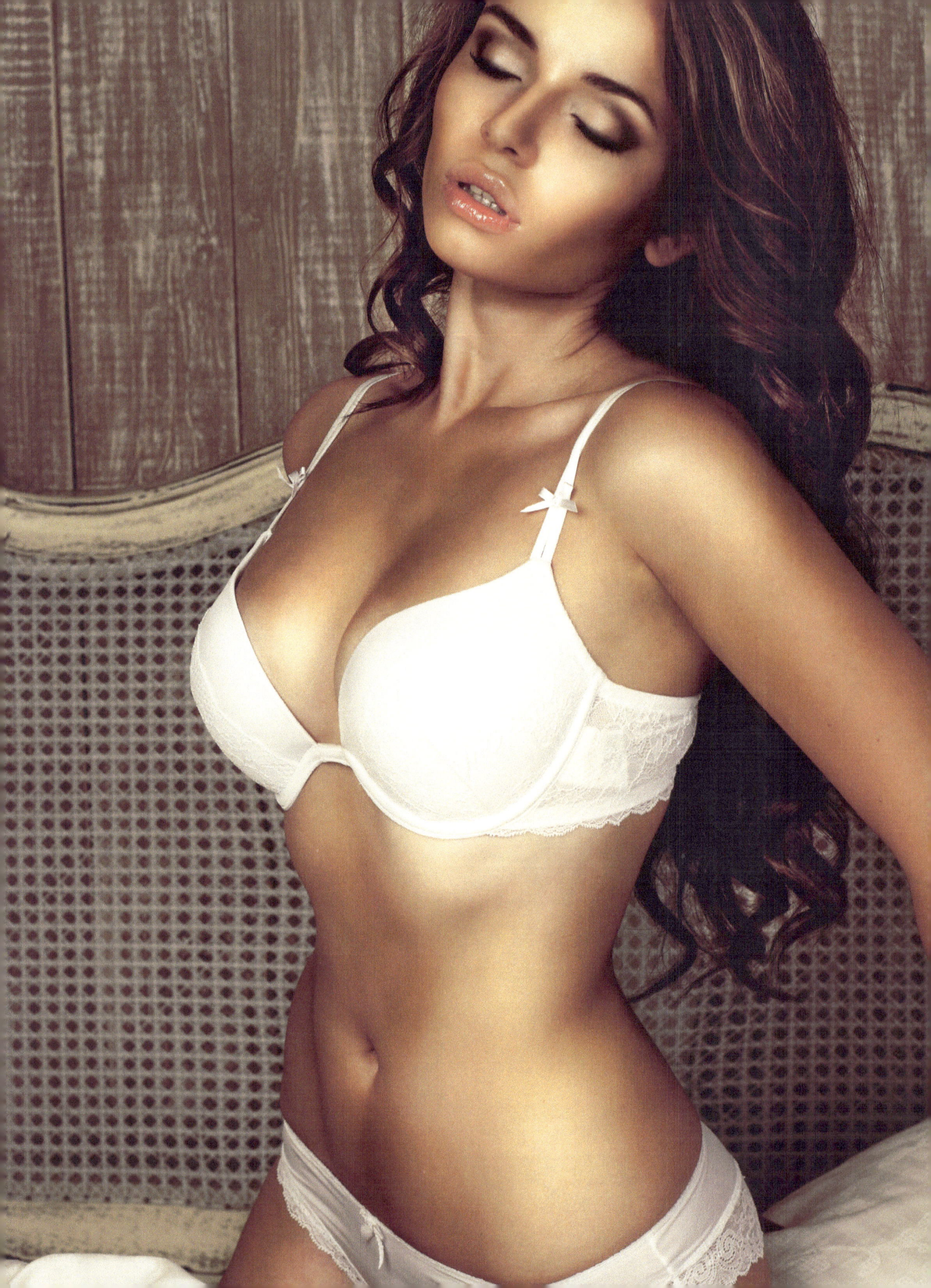

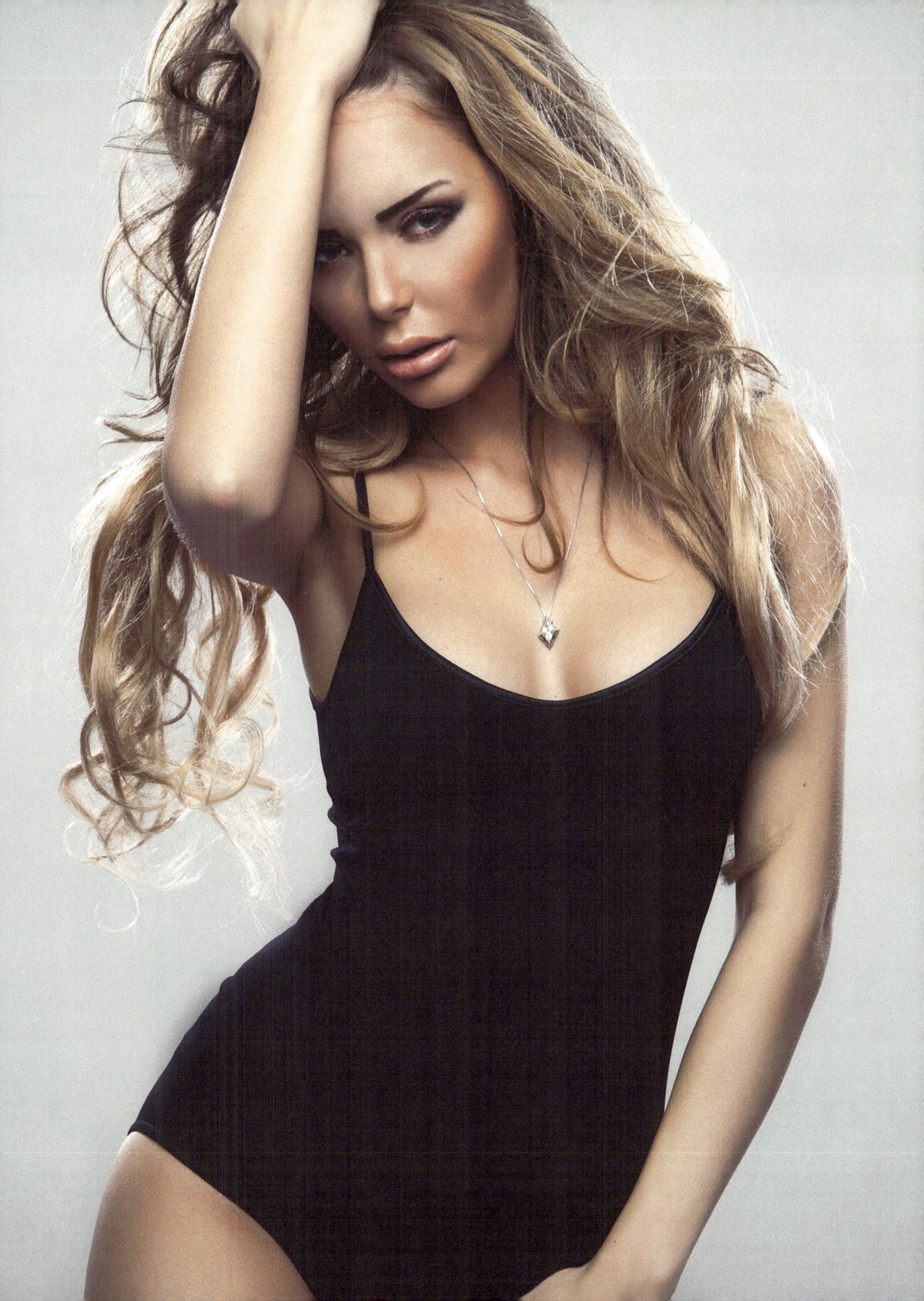

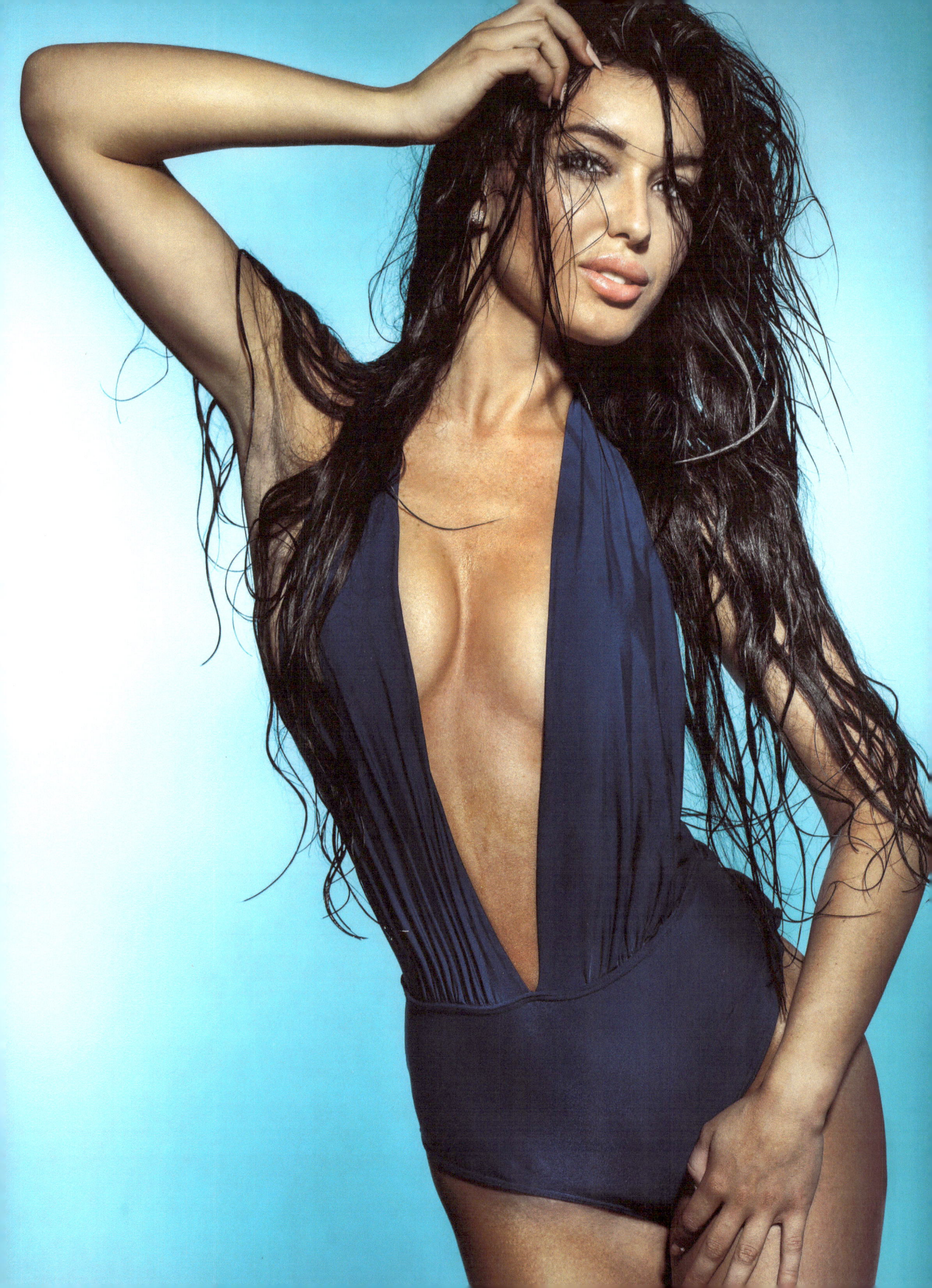

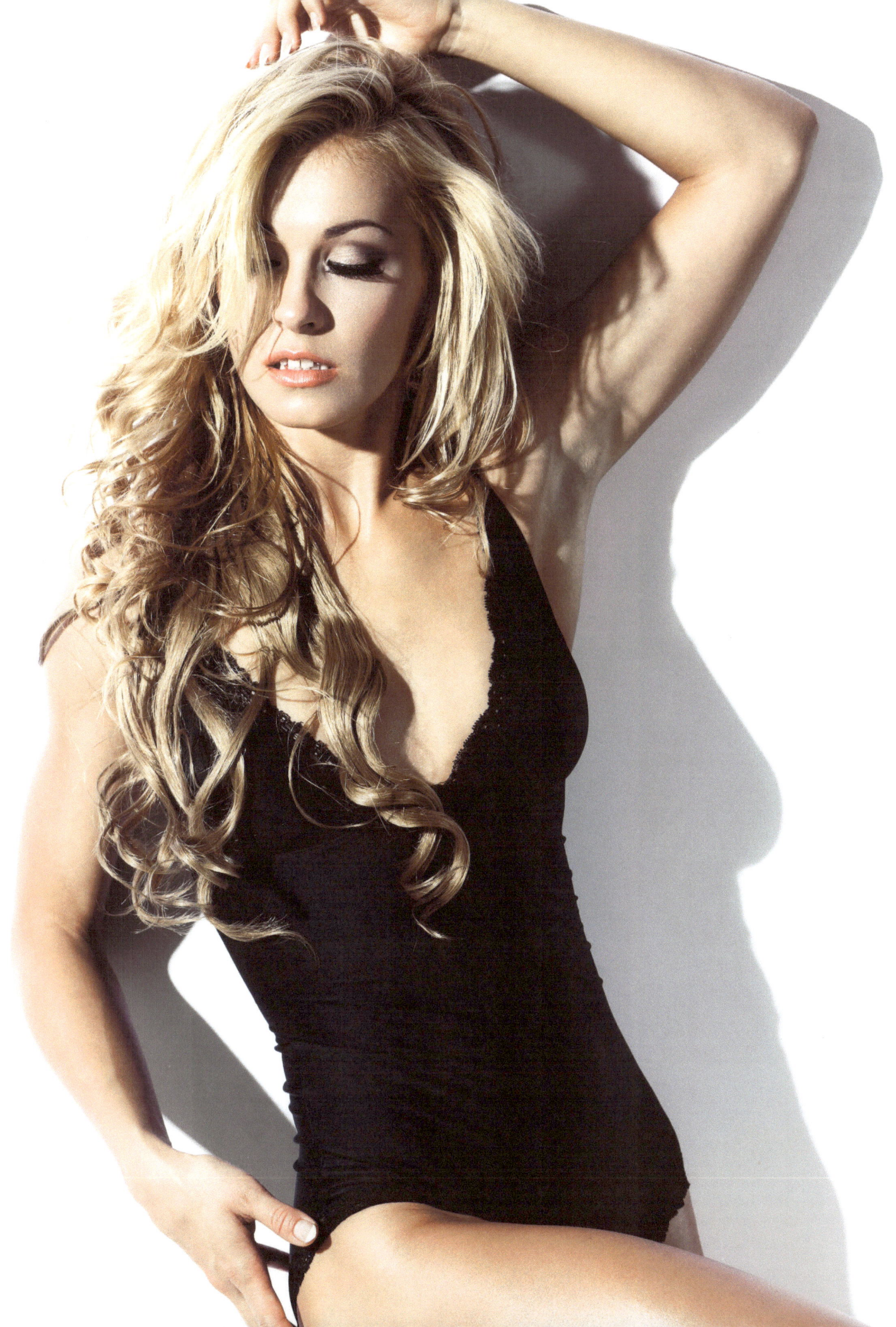

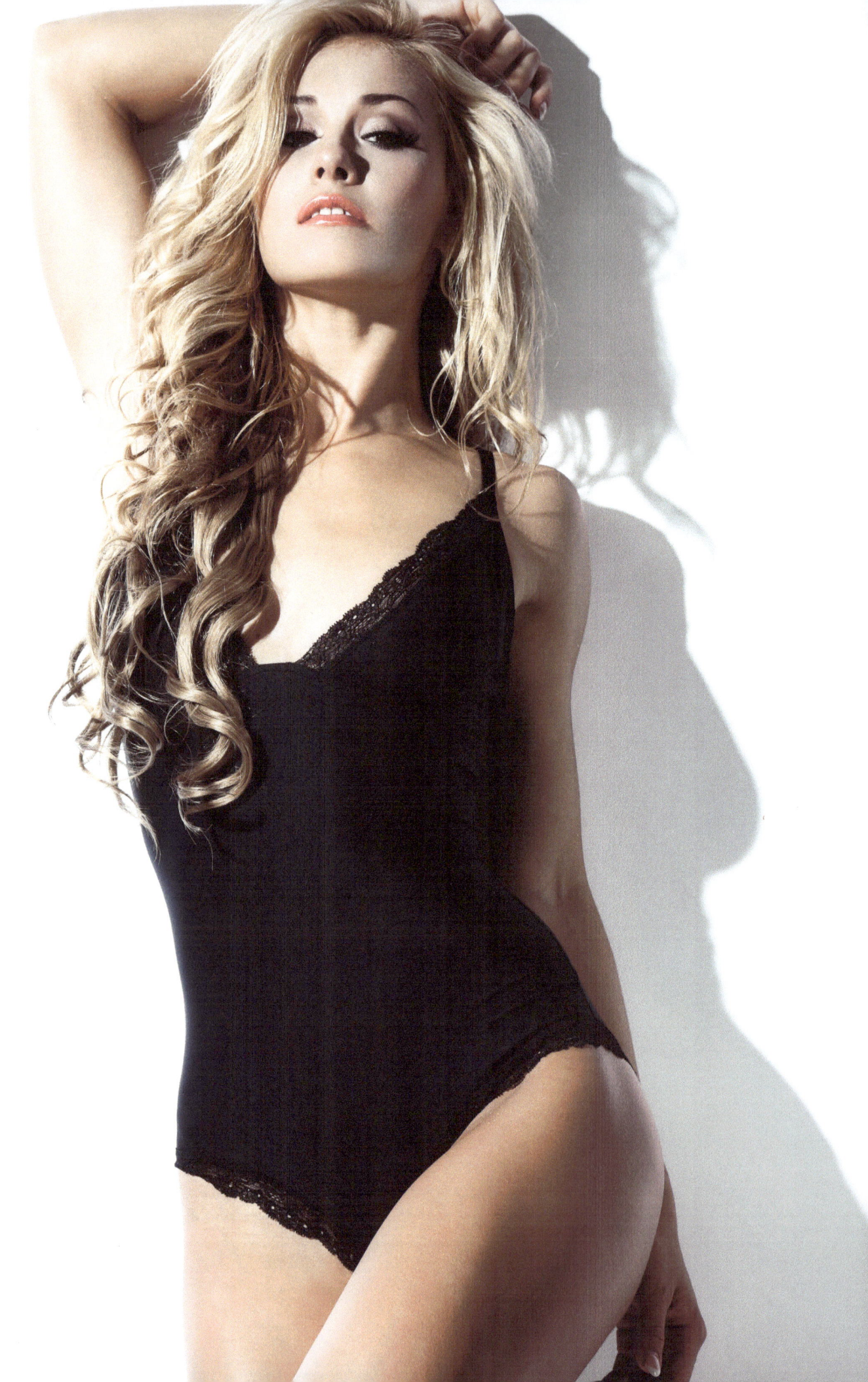

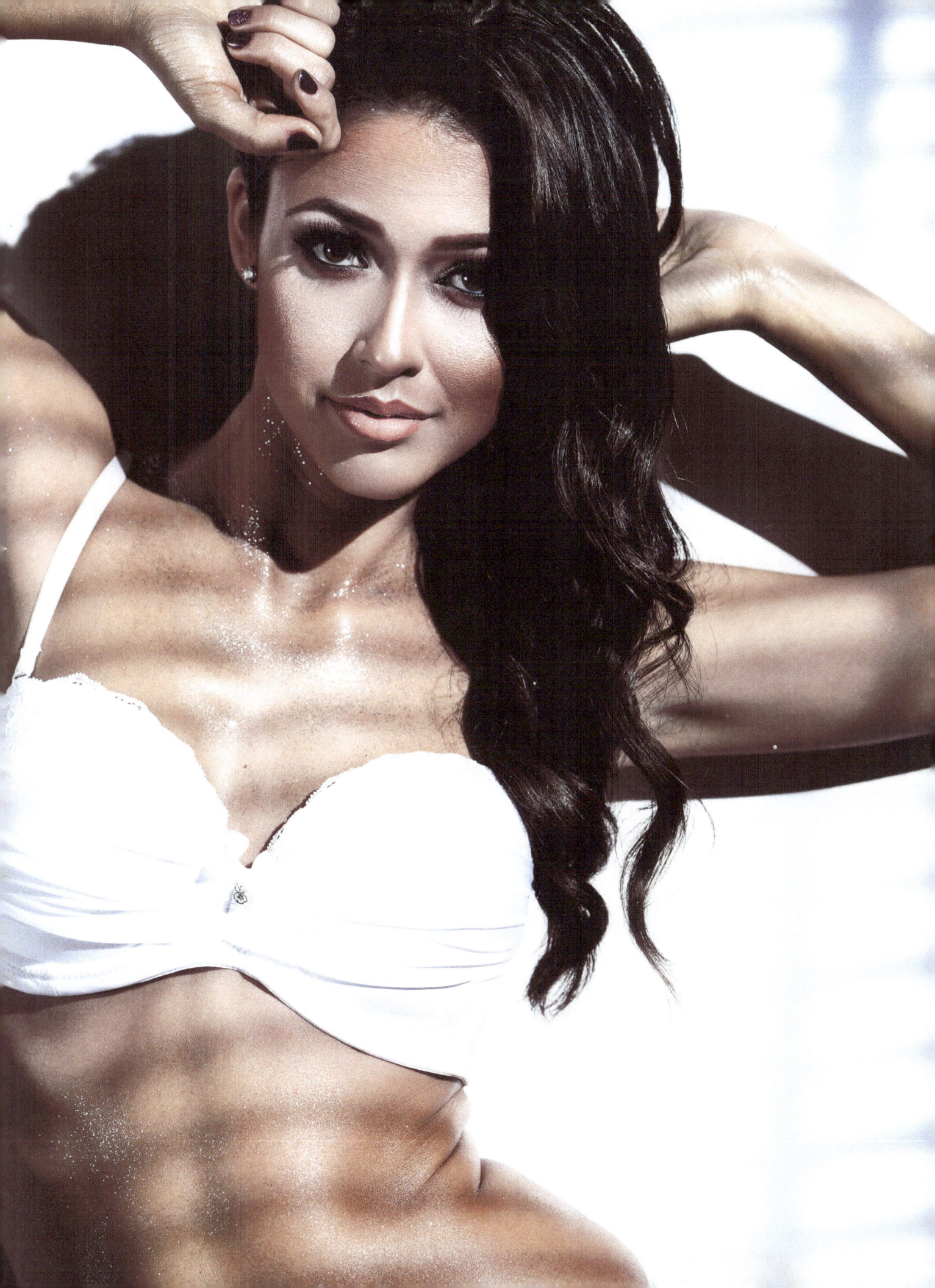

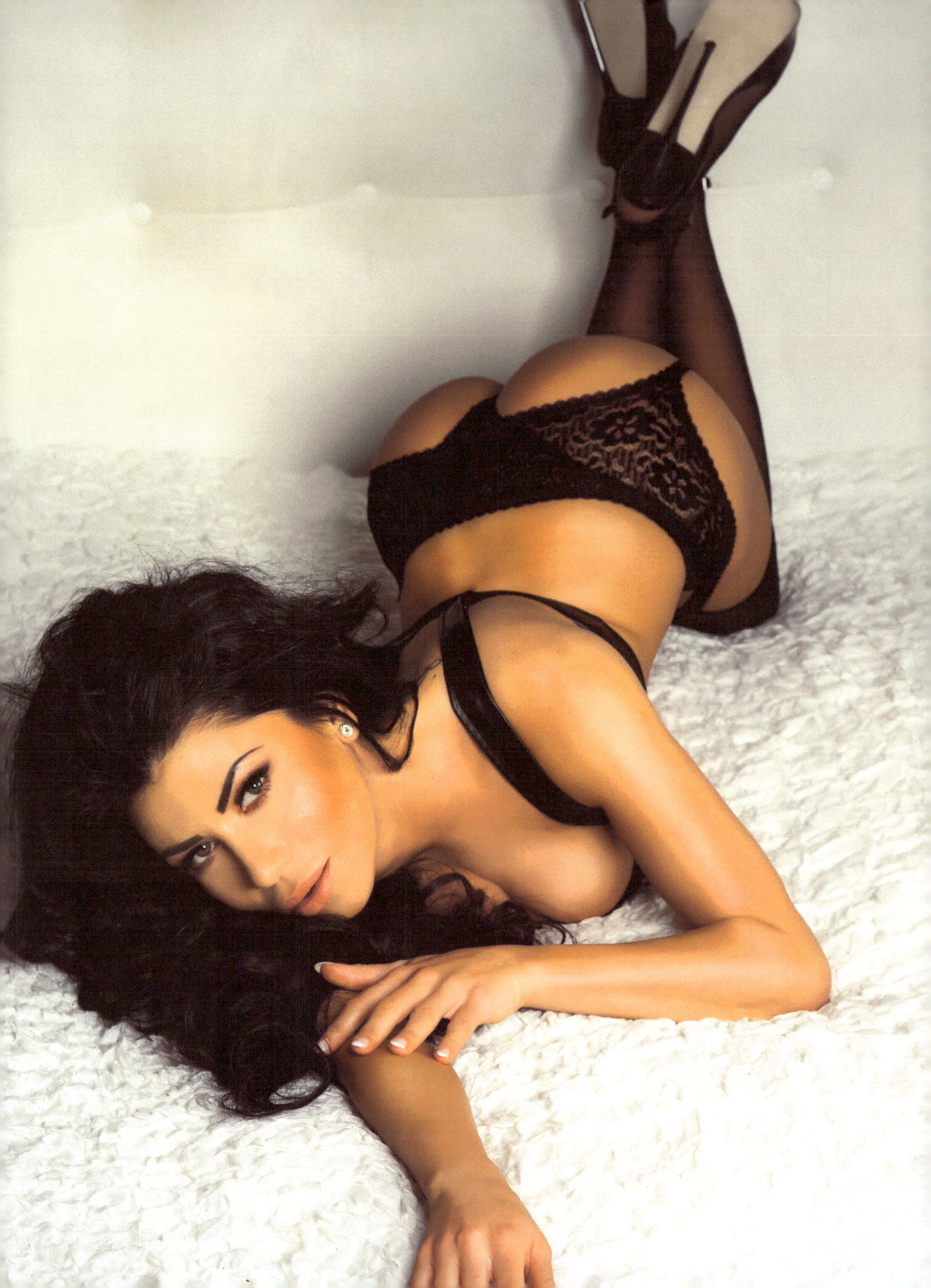

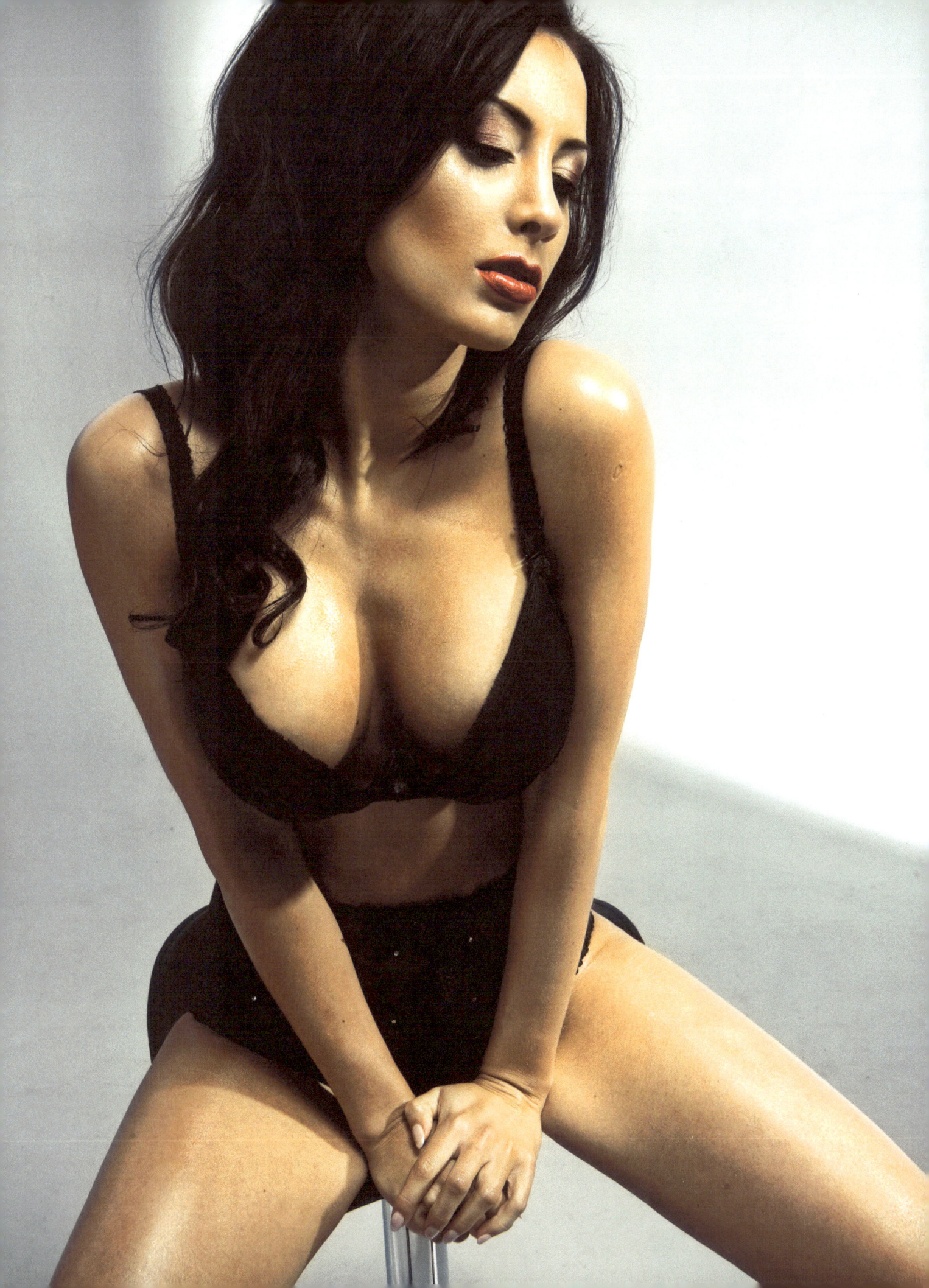

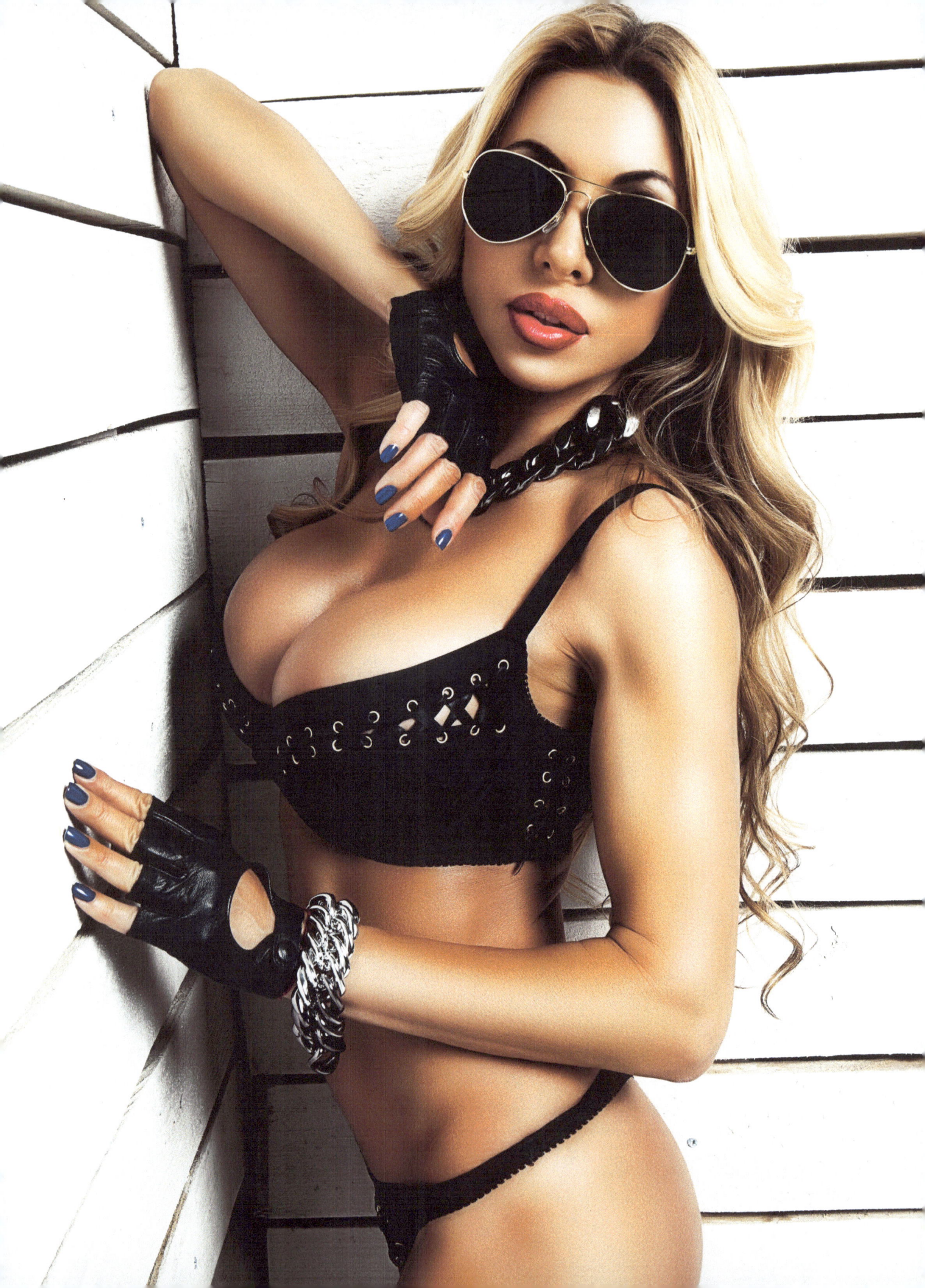

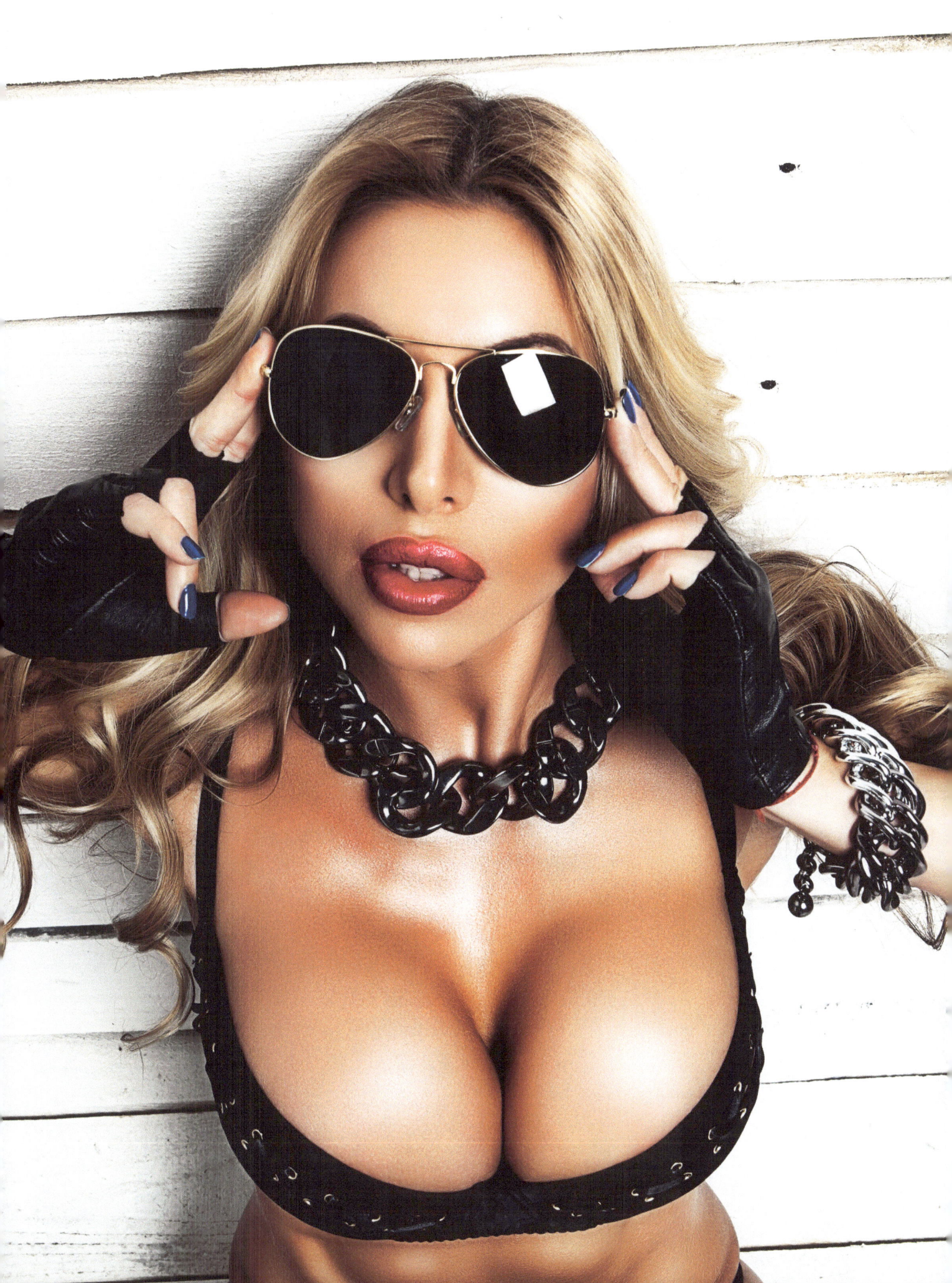

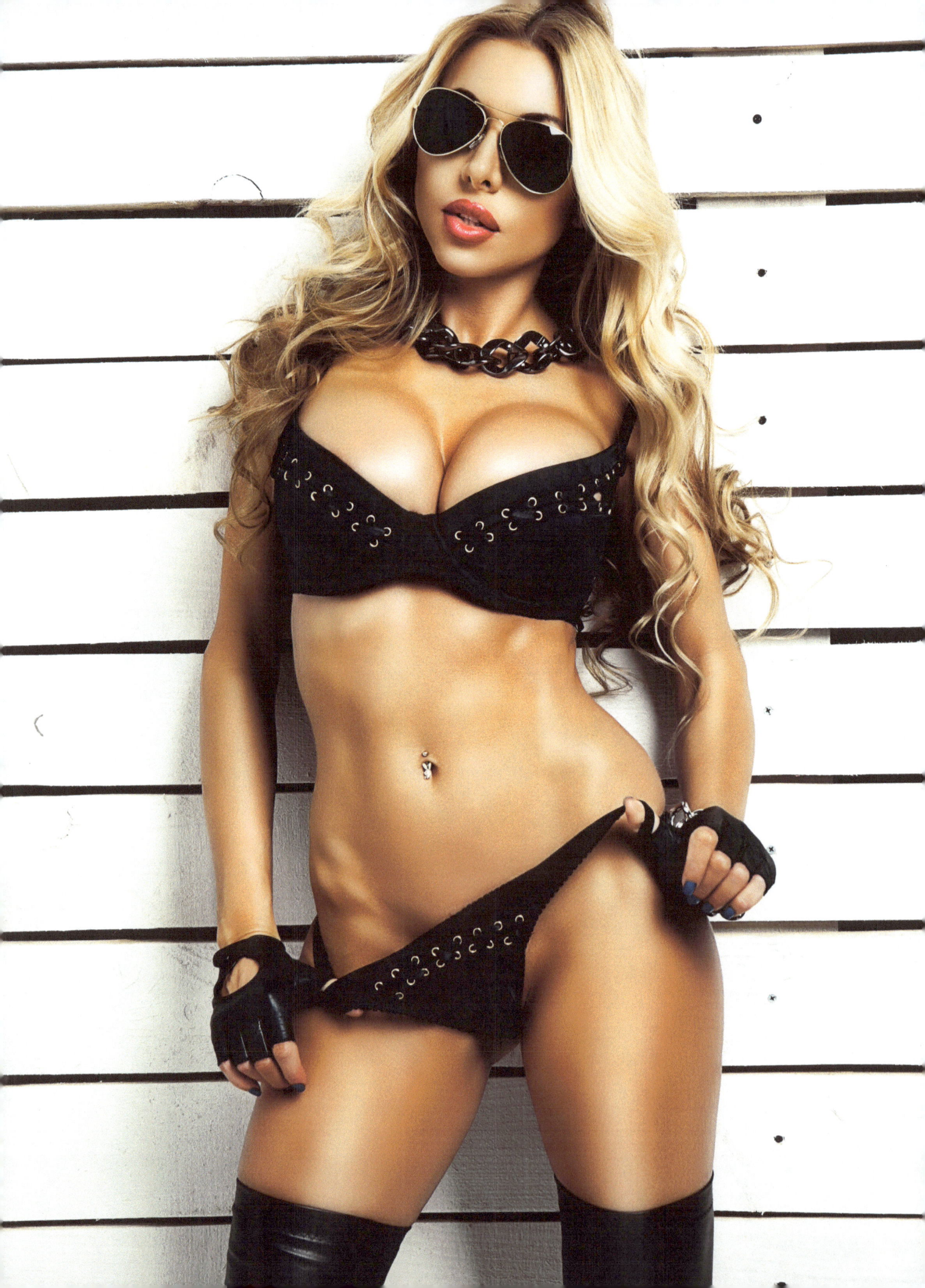

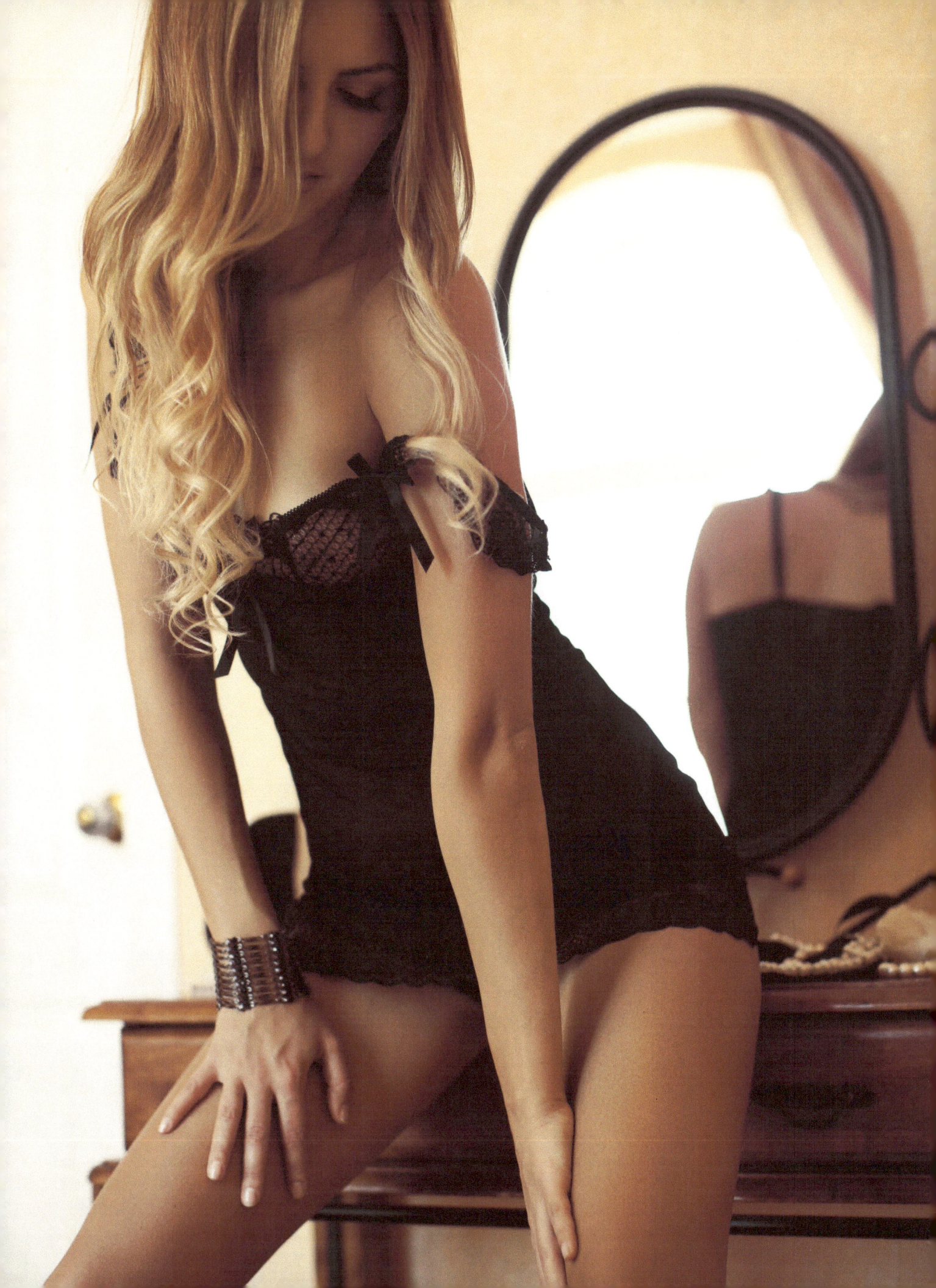

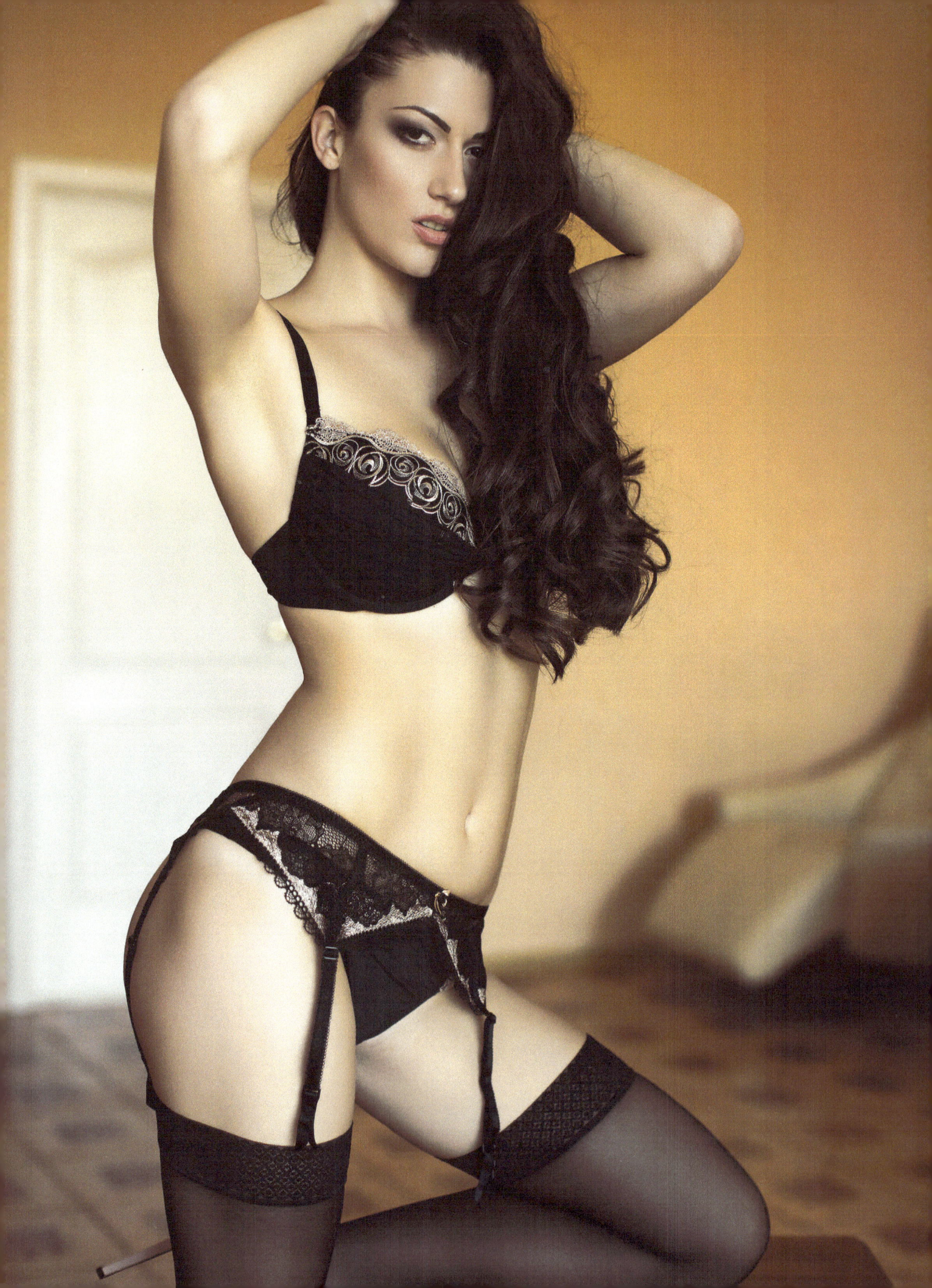

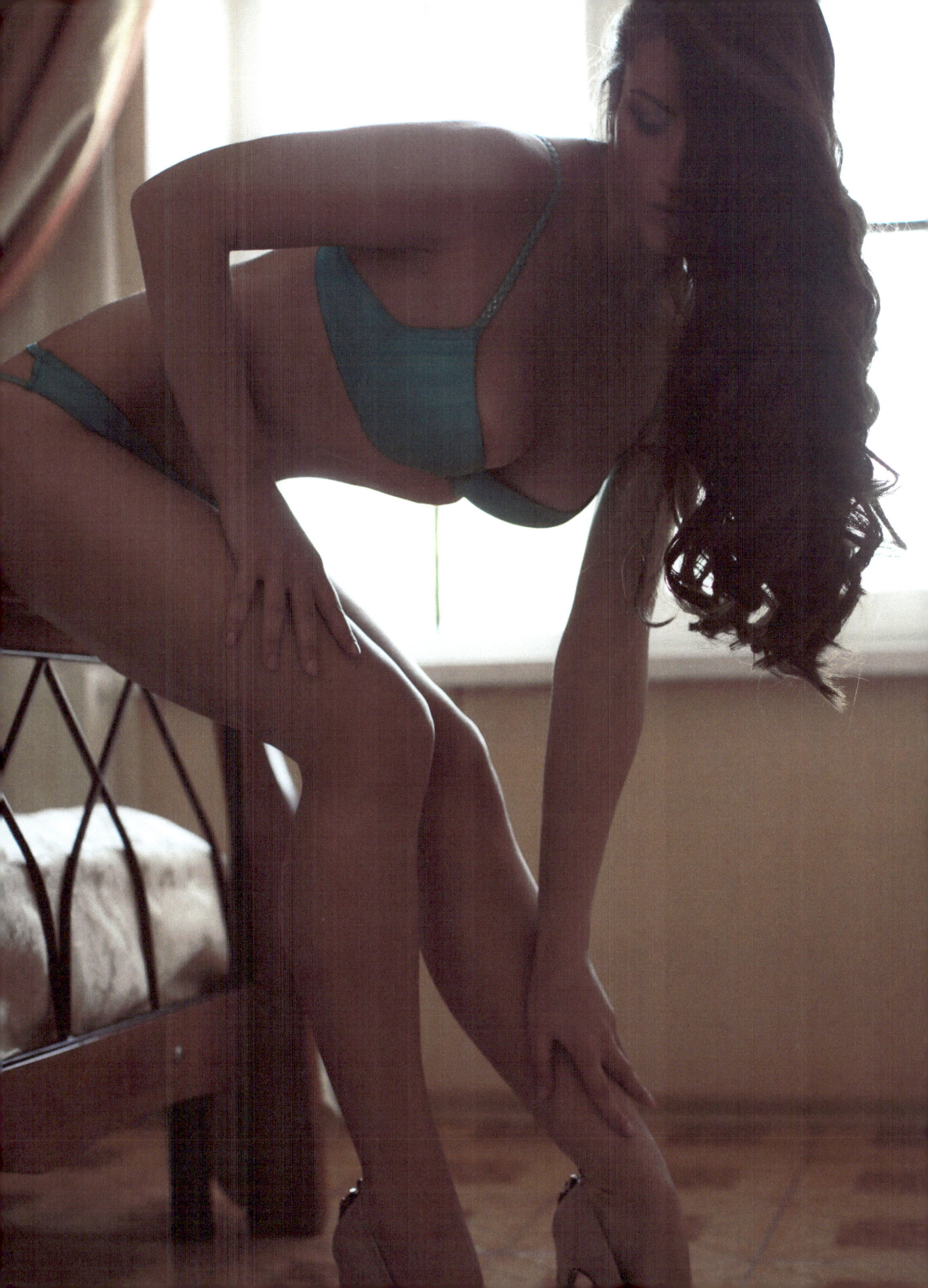

www.ingramcontent.com/pod-product-compliance
Lightning Source LLC
Chambersburg PA
CBHW050420180526

45159CB00005B/2341